World War

Potato

By Dave Villager

An introduction by the author

Hello, Dave the human here! I thought I'd better give this book an introduction because it's a bit weird. First of all, this book doesn't contain any real spoilers for the *Dave the Villager* series. However, if you haven't read the entire series up to book 40, there may be some references that you don't understand.

As I said, this is a bit of a weird book. A while back, I had an idea: what if Carl and Alex, two main characters from the *Dave the Villager* series, wrote an action movie together? Anyone who's read the main series will know that Alex and Carl often work on comic books together, and many of their ideas are absolutely ridiculous. Now you get to see what would happen if the two of them wrote a proper book. And, as you might expect, it is a bit crazy.

Anyway, this is a bit of an odd book; maybe no one else will find it funny apart from me. Still, I hope you enjoy it!

Dave the human, December 2021

An introduction by Carl

Sometimes, a book comes along that is so awesome and cool that it changes the face of literature. This is one such book. People used to say that creepers couldn't write books because we don't have hands, but I proved them all wrong. This book in front of you will change your life. It will make you laugh; it will make you cry; it will make you think. I warn you, once you read this book, you will never be the same again. So, prepare to be amazed. Oh, and if you stole this book, I will find you and blow you to bits! No one messes with Carl the creeper.

An introduction by Alex

Hi, I hope you like our book! Byyyyyyyyye!!!

CHAPTER ONE

Dastardly Dave

Detective Carl McCarl woke up, got out of bed, and then made himself some mushroom stew for breakfast. Then he got dressed, putting his pants on first, then his shirt, then his —

Alex, what are you doing?

Oh, hi Carl. I'm just writing the first chapter of our book.

I can see that. Why are you showing Detective Carl McCarl getting ready?

Because that's what he does. He wakes up, gets ready, and then he goes to work.

I know that, but it's not a very exciting way to start the story, Alex.

Oh, sorry, Carl. Do you want to start instead?

I thought you'd never ask. Here's how you start a story...

BOOOOOOOOOOOOOOOOOOOMMMMMMMMMMMM!!!!!!!!!!!!!!!

An explosion exploded. It was the biggest, coolest explosion in the whole world, but Detective Carl McCarl didn't care. He was so cool that even as the explosion exploded behind him, he didn't turn around. Instead, he just put on his sunglasses and said:

"Check, please."

Alex, don't interrupt me while I'm writing!

Sorry, Carl. But I don't understand – why did Detective Carl McCarl say "check, please"?

Because it's a cool catchphrase. Catchphrases don't have to make sense!

Oh, I didn't know that. I wish I could be a great writer like you, Carl.

Well, we can't all be geniuses. Anyway, let me continue the story...

"Thank you for saving us from the explosion, Detective Carl," said the orphan villager children. "But Dastardly Dave is getting away!"

"Don't worry," said Detective Carl McCarl. "Dastardly Dave has an appointment. An appointment with my fist in his face."

"You're so cool, Carl!" The orphans shouted.

Detective Carl McCarl put on his sunglasses.

Um, Carl, wasn't Detective Carl McCarl already wearing sunglasses?

Well, he's wearing two pairs now. Two pairs of sunglasses are extra cool.

Good point, Carl. Sorry, I'll let you get on with the story now.

Detective Carl McCarl ran as fast as his legs could carry him. Which was pretty fast as he was really athletic and handsome. He ran across the roof of the skyscraper and could see Dastardly Dave climbing into his flying minecart.

"Ha ha ha, you'll never catch me, Detective McCarl!" Dastardly Dave laughed.

Detective McCarl started running even faster than he had been running before, which was pretty fast. Dastardly Dave and his pet pig Spidroth took off in their flying minecart, but Carl McCarl jumped off the side of the skyscraper and grabbed the edge of the minecart just in time. All the people down below on the street all cheered and told McCarl that he was cool.

Dastardly Dave pulled out a sword and tried to hit Carl's hands to make him let go, but Carl was too fast for him. He swung himself up into the minecart using his super-strong muscles, then pulled out his own sword, pointing it at dastardly Dave. Spidroth the pig cowered in terror because she was a big coward.

Dastardly Dave swung his sword at Carl, but Carl was too quick for him. He blocked the blow, then chopped off Dastardly Dave's sword hand. The hand and the sword both went flying off the minecart, down to the street below.

"Need a hand?" Detective McCarl asked with a sly grin.

"Even though I've just lost my hand and I'm in a significant amount of pain, I have to admire how funny that joke was," said Dastardly Dave, scowling. "I surrender."

"Oink," whimpered Spidroth the pig.

"I want a name," growled Detective McCarl, pointing his sword at Dastardly Dave. "I know you only work for money. Who hired you to blow up that orphanage?"

Dastardly Dave grinned. "You wouldn't believe me if I told you."

"Try me."

"It was Doctor Boggo," said Dastardly Dave. "Your old nemesis."

"Doctor Boggo is dead," said McCarl. "I killed him myself. I chopped off his head, and then he fell into a lake of lava and then the lava was blown up with TNT, and then more lava fell on top of it."

"You think that's enough to kill Doctor Boggo?" grinned Dastardly Dave. "He's back, Detective McCarl. And he has big plans for the city of Awesomeville."

Carl!

What is it, Alex?

You can't have Detective Carl McCarl kick a suspect and a pet pig off a flying minecart. I thought he was meant to be a hero?

Yeah, but he's a cool hero. He sometimes does bad things to get the job done.

Still, it does seem a bit mean.

Okay, okay, I'll change it. Some people have no respect for art...

Detective McCarl karate kicked Dastardly Dave and Spidroth the pig, and they both went flying. They landed safely in a swimming pool, and neither of them died.

"Talk about making a splash," grinned McCarl, putting on his sunglasses.

12

He went to the control panel and flew the flying minecart back to his luxurious skyscraper apartment. But when he got there, there was no sign of his dog or his potato wife.

"Dog!" McCarl shouted. "Potato wife!"

Then he went into the kitchen and saw a piece of paper on the counter. It was a note:

Dear Carl, said the note, *this is your dog and your potato wife. We've left you, and we're not coming back. All you care about is your police work. We know you are a true hero, and this city needs you, but we need you too. We can't go on like this anymore. We're both sorry. Yours sincerely, your dog and your potato wife.*

"NOOOOOOOOOOOOOOOOOOOOOOOOOOOOOOOOOOOOOOOOOOOOOO!!!!!! !!!!!!!!" he bellowed.

Suddenly his redstone radio crackled into life.

"Come in, Detective McCarl!" said a voice over the radio. "Detective McCarl, please return to the station, old chap!"

McCarl sighed. The life of a cop was a tough one. It was a full-time job, with no time for family life. Detective McCarl had lost track of how many dogs and potato wives had left him over the years. He wanted to be a good husband and dog owner, but the job had to come first. The safety of the people of Awesomeville had to come first.

Carl pressed the button on the side of the radio. "I'm on my way, Chief," he said, putting on his sunglasses. "Detective McCarl is on the case."

Wow, Carl, that was really cool.

Thanks, Alex.

But it was a bit sad when Detective McCarl's wife and dog left him. Wouldn't it be nicer if they didn't leave?

Alex, good stories need drama. Detective McCarl is so committed to his job that his personal life suffers. It makes him cooler that way.

I guess so. Carl, can I write the next chapter, please?

Er, I suppose so. But don't make it too nice. Detective stories need lots of death and horrible things to happen. It needs to be gritty.

Okay, I'll do my best. Thanks, Carl. Also, can I have a bite of your baked potato?

No.

CHAPTER TWO

You're Partners!

Detective Carl McCarl opened the door of the police station then walked into the police station with his legs and feet. There were lots of other people in the police station, but he walked past them to the door of the office of the police chief, whose name was Chief Porkins. Detective McCarl knocked on the door, and Chief Porkins told him to come in.

"Hi Detective McCarl, it's really, really good to see you," said Chief Porkins.

"Thanks, Chief Porkins, said Detective McCarl. "You're my best friend."

"You're my best friend too," said Chief Porkins.

Then Detective Carl McCarl and Chief Porkins hugged each other.

HUG!

I'm writing the second chapter of the book.

I don't want to be rude, but this is awful. Detective stories are meant to be gritty. Everyone has to be angry all the time – and there should never be any hugging!

Sorry, Carl. Do you want to take over?

I will, thanks. Let me show you how it's done...

Detective Carl McCarl barged into Chief Porkins's office, kicking the door down.

"Detective McCarl, you're late, old chap," growled Chief Porkins.

"Shove it up your cakehole, Chief," growled Detective McCarl. "While you've been sitting here behind your big fancy desk, I was out on the streets catching criminals."

"Don't take that tone with me, old chap!" Chief Porkins shouted, banging a trotter on the desk. "I was out fighting crime when you were still in diapers!"

"Yeah, well, that was a long time ago, wasn't it?" said Detective McCarl. "Now you just sit behind a desk eating pumpkin pie all day. You don't know what it's like, on those mean streets. Every day I'm fighting off exploding creepers and zombies who want to eat my brains. This city is one bad day away from total destruction. It's only cops like me who hold back the tide."

Chief Porkins slammed his trotter on the desk again. "I've had it with your attitude, McCarl! You're a maverick! A loose cannon! Yes, you're a jolly good cop, but I hate your guts!"

"I hate your guts too, chief," growled Detective McCarl.

"Good, then we're in agreement. Now, it's been five months since your last partner, Little Billy, was eaten by killer rabbits."

"A bad way to go," growled Detective McCarl.

"Anyway, old bean, you'll be pleased to hear that I've found you a new partner."

Detective Carl McCarl growled even more than he'd been growling before. "I work alone," he said.

"Not anymore, dear chap," said Chief Porkins.

The door swung open, and in walked a girl with pale skin and bright orange hair.

"This is Junior Detective Alex," said Chief Porkins. "She's your new partner."

"So, you're the famous Carl McCarl," said Junior Detective Alex, shooting him a nasty look. "Shouldn't an old man like you be retired by now?"

"Shouldn't a young idiot like you still be in school?" growled Detective Carl McCarl.

"Enough!" yelled Chief Porkins, slamming both his trotters on the desk. "You two deserve each other! You're partners!"

"Er, you already said that, Chief," said Detective McCarl.

"Oh yeah," said Chief Porkins. "Now, get out of my office."

Oh, Carl?

Yes, Alex?

Can Alex McAlex be a bit nicer? She seemed a bit mean.

Okay, okay, you can write the lines for Detective McAlex.

Oh, thank you, thank you, thank you!

All right, let's get on with this, or this book will never get written.

Carl, shall we move on to the next chapter?

No, we can't yet. Every chapter has to end on an awesome cliffhanger to keep people reading.

Oh, nice! Can I come up with a cliffhanger this time?

Er, I guess so.

Thaaaaaank you!

Detective Carl McCarl and Junior Detective McAlex walked outside the police station to see if any crimes were being committed. Then, before they could do anything else, a giant pig appeared, stomping across the city and crushing all the buildings.

"Oh no!" Detective Carl McCarl shouted. "It's Pigzilla!"

CHAPTER THREE

The Pigger They Are, The Porker They Fall

Pigzilla? Really? That's the best cliffhanger idea you could come up with, Alex?

Don't you think it's cool? It's a giant pig!

Yes, I gathered that. Okay, so what happens next?

Okay, here goes...

Pigzilla stomped across the city, but thankfully he was really, really careful not to tread on anyone, so no one got squished. Then Detective Carl McCarl and Junior Detective Alex McAlex made friends with Pigzilla, and they all shared a big pumpkin pie and were best friends forever. The end.

Alex, what kind of stupid story is this?? Why is Pigzilla making friends instead of eating people?

Oh, sorry, Carl. I just didn't think it would be very nice if Pigzilla hurt anybody.

Giant monsters are supposed to hurt people. That's what they do! Let me show you how it's done...

Pigzilla, the giant pig monster, stomped through the city, destroying buildings and frying people with his inferno breath. Everyone was screaming and running for cover. An old lady spotted Detective Carl McCarl and said:

"Help us, Detective McCarl! We need someone awesome and heroic to save us from the monster!"

"Never fear, you old bag," said Detective McCarl. "By the time I'm finished with that monster, it will be nothing but porkchops."

Carl, don't forget that Detective McAlex has to help too.

Okay, okay...

"Oh, and my partner Alex McAlex will be helping as well," said Detective McCarl. "She might not be as cool as me, but we're both police officers, and we'll get the job done."

Can I still write the lines for Detective McAlex, Carl?

Yeah, all right.

Yay!

"Don't worry, kind old lady," said Detective McAlex. "We'll stop Pigzilla's rampage and save the city. We know he's probably a good guy deep inside. We'll try and become his best friend."

"Er, maybe," said Detective McCarl. "But if he's an evil monster, we'll definitely kill him."

"We'll either kill him or become his best friends," said Detective McAlex. "It will be one of those two options."

"Notch bless you, dears," said the old lady.

Detective McCarl and Junior Detective McAlex ran forward, following the path of destruction that Pigzilla was leaving. The city of Awesomeville was on fire, and people were running for their lives. A few of them stopped to get Detective McCarl's autograph, but then they kept running.

Pigzilla was a pig monster that stood on its hind legs. Its mouth was full of razor-sharp teeth, and it could breathe jets of purple fire. Every time it took a step, the ground shook, and buildings crumbled. Detective McCarl knew that he would need all his ninja skills to defeat the monster, but he knew he could do it because he was so cool and awesome.

"Down here, you big pig idiot!" Detective McCarl yelled up at Pigzilla. The monster turned and looked down at him, its eyes glowing with purple fire.

"Hi, Pigzilla!" said Detective McAlex. "We can see you're angry, so we wanted to talk to you to see if we can help. If you want, we can all be friends?"

"ROOOOOOOOOOOOOOOOOOOOOAAAAAAAAAAAAAAAAAAAARRRRRRR RRRRRRRRRRRRRRRRRR!!!!!!!!!!!!!!!!!!!!!!!!!!!!" said Pigzilla.

"I think that's a no," said Detective McCarl.

Pigzilla opened its mouth and fired a jet of purple fire right at them. McCarl and McAlex had to dive out of the way to avoid getting roasted.

"Do you still think Pigzilla's gonna be your best friend?" Detective McCarl shouted.

"I still trust in the power of friendship," said Detective McAlex. "Pigzilla! Listen to me! Do you want me to bake you a nice pumpkin pie, and then we can read comic books together?"

Pigzilla fired another jet of purple fire down at the ground, and McCarl and McAlex quickly ran down an alleyway between two buildings for cover.

"I've got a plan," said Detective McCarl. "We need to build two TNT cannons on different roofs. You fire one, and I'll fire the other. Then we keep firing TNT at that monster until it goes down."

"I've got a better idea," said McAlex. "Why don't we give it some cake?"

Detective McCarl gave her a funny look.

"How's that going to help?"

"Everyone loves cake," shrugged McAlex. "Apart from people who don't like cake or people who are allergic to cake."

Detective McCarl rolled his eyes and sighed wearily.

"We don't have time for this," he growled.

"Let's just give it a chance," said Detective McAlex. "I'll bake a delicious cake and give it to Pigzilla, and hopefully, he'll become my best friend."

"Or he'll eat you," said McCarl.

"Yes, either he'll become my best friend, or he'll eat me. It will definitely be one of those two options."

McAlex quickly pulled out a crafting table and placed it down on the ground. Then she reached into her pockets and pulled out three sheaves of wheat, two piles of sugar, one egg, and three buckets of milk.

Alex, how can Detective McAlex fit three buckets of milk inside her pockets?

Um... She has magical pockets.

Riiiiight.

Detective McAlex finished the recipe, and a cake appeared on the crafting table.

"Mmm, cake!" she said, lifting the cake up towards her mouth.

"Er, I thought you were supposed to be offering the cake to Pigzilla?" said Detective McCarl.

"Oh yeah," said McAlex. She walked out of the alleyway, holding the cake up in front of her.

"Pigzilla! Look what I've got for you! Delicious cake!"

Pigzilla opened its mouth and blasted Detective McAlex to smithereens with purple fire.

"RIP Detective McAlex," said McCarl, taking off his sunglasses as a mark of respect. "You served the city well. I will avenge your tragic death."

Carl! You can't kill off Detective McAlex! She's one of the main characters!

What's wrong with killing off a main character? If you do that, it shows that no one is safe and that anyone could die at any moment. It's edgy and cool!

Please, Carl! Please can we keep Detective McAlex alive? PUH-LEEEEEEASE???

Okay, okay.

Detective McAlex walked out of the alleyway, holding the cake up in front of her.

"Pigzilla!" she shouted. "Look what I've got for you! Delicious cake!"

Pigzilla licked his lips.

"Thank you, Detective McAlex, that's really nice of you. You're my best friend."

Alex!!!

What's the matter, Carl?

I thought Pigzilla was meant to be a ferocious monster? Ferocious monsters don't speak!

Oh, right, good point, Carl. I'll change it...

"Pigzilla!" shouted Detective McAlex. "Look what I've got for you! Delicious cake!"

Pigzilla licked his lips. Then he roared a happy roar. Detective McAlex couldn't understand what the roar meant, but she guessed that if Pigzilla could talk, he would have said:

"Thank you, Detective McAlex, that's really nice of you. You're my best friend."

Pigzilla reached down with one of his enormous trotters and took the cake. Then he opened his mouth and gobbled the cake down in one bite. He let out another happy roar and smiled at Detective McAlex.

"I think me and Pigzilla are now best friends," said McAlex.

"Er, that's great," said Detective McCarl. "But there's still a giant pig monster in the middle of the city. Are you sure we shouldn't blow it up with TNT?"

"Pigzilla, would you mind leaving the city?" asked McAlex. "I'm sorry to be rude, but you're a bit too big to be here. There's a nice plains biome to the west of here. You could go there? I'll come and see you tomorrow and bring you more cake."

Pigzilla let out another happy roar. Because Pigzilla was a monster, Alex couldn't understand what the roar meant, but she thought it must mean something like:

"Thank you, Detective McAlex. I'm very grateful for all you've done for me. I will leave the city of Awesomeville and go to the plains biome. I very much look forward to seeing you again and eating more of your delicious cake. You truly are the greatest friend a giant pig monster could have, and I appreciate your compassion and your dedication to using peaceful means instead of violence to resolve conflict. I love you very much, and I hope that we'll be best friends forever and ever."

Pigzilla stomped its way back across the city.

"We did it," said McAlex happily. "We saved the city!"

"For now," said Detective McCarl. "But there's always another crime to be solved. Another bad guy to be defeated."

"Another cake to be eaten," said McAlex.

Suddenly, Chief Porkins came running out of the police station.

"Chaps!" He shouted. "I say, chaps!"

"What is it, chief?" asked McAlex.

"There's been a break-in at the old potato factory."

Detective McCarl's mouth fell open in shock. "Please tell me the potatoes are okay, Chief. PLEASE TELL ME THE POTATOES ARE OKAY!!!"

"I'm afraid not, dear boy," said Chief Porkins solemnly. "All the potatoes in the factory have been stolen, and all the potatoes in every shop too. I'm afraid that Awesomeville... has completely run out of potatoes."

Suddenly it began to rain, and thunder streaked across the sky. Detective McCarl fell to his knees.

"NOOOOOOOOOOOOOOOOOOOOOOOOOOOOOOOOOOOOOOOOOOOOO OOOOOOOOOOO!!!!!!!!!!!!!!!!!!!!!"

CHAPTER FOUR

The Potato Factory

By the time Detective McCarl and McAlex arrived at the potato factory, it was swarming with police officers and police scientists in lab coats.

"Detective McCarl, it is good to see you," said Robo-Steve, the chief forensic investigator on the team. He was a gold robot who wore a long white lab coat.

"Cut the pleasantries," growled McCarl. "Tell me everything that you and our nerd buddies have found out so far."

As a super-tough police officer, Detective McCarl had little time for scientists and other geeks and nerds like that. All he cared about was catching criminals.

"Certainly, Detective," said Robo-Steve. "It seems that last night someone used TNT to blow a hole in the wall of the factory, and then a gang of criminals rushed in and stole all of the potatoes. Similar things happened across the city, all at the same time. Whoever orchestrated this must be some kind of criminal genius."

"Or maybe they just really wanted some baked potatoes," suggested Detective McAlex.

"Well, I hope they enjoy those potatoes while they can," grunted McCarl. "As they won't be having any more potatoes where they're going — prison."

"Actually, I believe that prisoners eat quite a lot of potatoes," said Robo-Steve. "So that statement is factually inaccurate, Detective McCarl."

"Enough with the nerd talk," said Detective McCarl. "Do we have any clues?"

"Only one," said Robo-Steve. "The thieves left this behind."

He pointed to a gold helmet on the floor. Detective McCarl knelt down next to the helmet.

"Only a noob would wear gold armor," he said thoughtfully "A noob... or a piglin. I think I know who stole the potatoes."

"Who?" McAlex asked.

"My old nemesis — Doctor Boggo."

Robo-Steve gave Detective McCarl a funny look. "Detective, I believe your logic must be faulty. Doctor Boggo is dead."

"No," growled Detective McCarl. "But I'm dead. Dead serious about catching him and putting him in jail."

"And I'm dead serious too," said Detective McAlex. "Dead serious about the fantastic deals at Cake World! This weekend, Cake World has a fantastic offer: all cakes are half price. That's right, half price! But don't delay – this amazing offer is only valid for this weekend, and once all the cakes are gone, they're gone! So come on down to your nearest Cake World and stock up on cakes. Chocolate cakes not included."

Alex, what was that??

Oh, sorry Carl, it was just a quick advert. Cake World said that if I mentioned their sale in this book, they'd give me one free cake!

You can't just put an advert in the middle of our book! This is meant to be a gritty detective story, not a promotion for cakes! If it was an ad for baked potatoes, I'd consider it, but cakes are stupid.

Sorry, Carl. Shall I change Detective McAlex's line?

Yes, you should.

Okay...

"And I'm dead serious too," said Detective McAlex. "I've heard there's a fantastic sale this weekend at Cake World, but I'm not going to mention it because I'm a serious detective and all I think about is solving crimes, not about the fact that all cakes at Cake World are half price this weekend. And I especially don't think about the fact that once all the cakes are gone, they're gone. Also, the thought that chocolate cakes are not included never even crosses my mind."

Is that better, Carl?

Yeah, whatever. Let's just get on with the story.

The two detectives went outside to get some fresh air.

"It's a tough job this," growled McCarl in a manly way. "In all my years as a cop on the mean streets, I've seen things ordinary people could never understand."

"Yesterday, I saw something I didn't understand," said McAlex. "I saw a salmon wearing a pair of shoes and walking down the street. Although it may have been a dream. Sometimes I get dreams and real life mixed up."

"Er, okay," said McCarl.

"Do you think salmon can speak?" asked McAlex.

"No, I don't."

"But maybe they have their own fishy language that only they understand."

"Let's stop talking about salmon."

"Okay," said McAlex. "Just one more question — do you think if a salmon went to the gym every day for ten years, it would be able to beat a ravager in a fight?"

Alex, why is Detective McAlex talking so much about salmon??

Sorry, Carl. Sometimes I start thinking about things, and I can't stop. Yesterday, I couldn't stop thinking about sponge blocks. They're so squishy. Have you ever squished a sponge block, Carl?

Can we just get on with the story, please?

Of course, sorry, sorry...

"As I was saying, it sure is tough being a cop," said Detective McCarl. "People think this job is all about catching bad guys, running away from explosions and putting on sunglasses, but that's only half the struggle. It takes a toll on your personal life. Did you know that my potato wife and my dog left me this morning?"

"I'm sorry to hear that," said McAlex. "I once dropped a piece of cake in a river. Thankfully, I was able to get the cake out, but by the time I did, it was really soggy and didn't taste very nice. It sure is tough being a cop."

Alex!!!

What now, Carl? Did I do something wrong?

Why is McAlex talking about dropping cake in a river?

Well, Detective McCarl was telling her a sad story, so I thought she should tell him a sad story as well.

Dropping a piece of cake in a river is not a sad story!

Okay, I'll try and come up with something sadder...

"I'm sorry to hear that," said McAlex. "I once dropped a piece of cake on a puppy's head, and it was so heavy that the puppy had to go to the hospital. Thankfully he was okay, but after that, he could never eat cake ever again. And that puppy's name... was Detective Alex McAlex. Yes, I was that puppy."

ALEX!!!!!!!!!!!!!!!!!!!!!!!!!!!

What's wrong, Carl? Was that story not sad enough?

No, it wasn't sad at all — it was just confusing and weird.

Okay, sorry, I'll try again...

"I'm sorry to hear that," said McAlex. "Lots of sad things have happened to me too. Once I saw a puppy crying, and I asked him why he was crying, and he said that he was allergic to cake, then I started crying too. Then all the other puppies in town started to cry, and that made all the people in town cry. There was so much crying that the town began to flood, and we all had to escape on boats, but because we kept crying, the water kept getting bigger and bigger until it was an entire ocean. And that ocean's name... was Detective Alex McAlex. Yes, I was that ocean."

Was that better, Carl?

Let's... Let's just go to the next chapter...

CHAPTER FIVE

The Old Goat

The Old Goat was a bar on the rough side of town. As Detective Carl McCarl and Detective Alex McAlex walked through the doors, everyone turned to look at them. Carl recognized many of the faces staring back at him: criminals he'd arrested in the past.

"This place looks nice," said Detective McAlex, smiling.

McCarl walked up to the bar.

"Detective McCarl," grunted the illager bartender. "To what do we owe this pleasure?"

"I'm looking for information," McCarl grunted back. "But first, my partner and I need a drink."

The bartender placed two buckets of milk on the bar. Detective McCarl picked up his bucket and took a sip. It was warm, but he was so thirsty that he didn't care.

"Now," said McCarl to the bartender, "tell me everything you know about Doctor Boggo."

"Doctor Boggo is dead," said the bartender, a little too quickly.

"Sure he is," grinned McCarl. He turned around to face all the criminals itting at their tables.

"One hundred emeralds to anyone who can tell me where Doctor Boggo s," Carl announced to the bar.

There were lots of shifty looks between the criminals, but no one said nything.

"Fine," said McCarl. "I tried to do this the nice way, but now I'm going to ave to do it the hard way." He pulled out a tiny TNT block from his pocket nd placed it in the middle of the floor, where it grew to full-size.

"What are you doing??" one of the criminals shouted.

McCarl grinned and pulled some flint and steel from his pocket.

"Either one of you tells me Doctor Boggo's location, or in ten seconds, we ll get blown to pieces. What's it gonna be?"

"You're bluffing," another criminal muttered.

"Am I?" grinned McCarl. "Ten... Nine..."

Wow, Carl, this is really exciting! Is Detective McCarl really going to blow up everyone in the bar?

I'm glad you like it, Alex. No, he won't need to, as one of the criminals will give him the information before he finishes the countdown.

Ah, cool. But what if one of the criminals didn't tell him? Would he actually light the TNT and blow himself and Detective McAlex up along with all criminals?

I guess not, but it doesn't matter, as he knows that one of the criminals will give him the information he needs. The criminals know Detective Carl McCarl isn't bluffing because he's such a rogue and a maverick — he's a police officer who doesn't play by the rules.

Wow, that's so cool. Maybe Detective McAlex shouldn't play by the rules either.

No, that wouldn't work, Alex. You can't have two police officers who don't play by the rules. You need one who doesn't play by the rules and another who does play by the rules so that they can argue all the time.

Wait, why do they need to argue all the time?

Because that's good drama.

Right, I think I understand now, Carl.

Good. Now let's get back to the story...

All the criminals around the room began to look terrified.

"Eight..." said McCarl. "Seven..."

"Don't worry, everyone," said Detective McAlex. "Detective McCarl isn't really going to light that TNT block. He's just doing it to scare you, but if the countdown reaches zero, he's not really going to do it."

Alex, what are you doing? Why is Detective McAlex being such an idiot?

She's not being an idiot, Carl; she's playing by the rules. I don't think police officers are allowed to blow up people with TNT. Plus, I thought you wanted the two detectives to argue all the time?

Okay, okay, let's get on with it...

"I'm not bluffing," McCarl told the criminals. "If you don't tell me where Doctor Boggo is, I'll blow us all to kingdom come."

"He is bluffing," said McAlex. "But we would still be very grateful if you would tell us where Doctor Boggo is."

"Okay," said the bartender, "I'll tell you what I know if you two both get out of my bar."

McCarl grinned. "That wasn't so hard, was it?"

"All I know is that there's an abandoned warehouse in the iron farming district. People say that Doctor Boggo's piglins often come in and out of the warehouse at night."

"Thanks," said Detective McCarl. He went over and picked up his TNT block, placing it back into his pocket. Then he and McAlex headed towards the door.

"Detective McCarl, don't you think we should pay for our buckets of milk?" McAlex asked.

Before McCarl could say anything, she ran back to the bar and handed the surprised bartender some emeralds.

"Keep the change," she said happily.

"But you haven't given me enough money," said the bartender.

"That's okay," said McAlex. "You can keep the change."

"But there is no change," said the bartender. "So, how can I keep it?"

"Oh," said McAlex. "Well, that's all the emeralds I've got, sorry!"

She and Detective McCarl left the bar and headed back onto the street. They were in the rough part of town, and there were criminals on every street corner. A group of iron golems were listening to a jukebox outside without a permit, but Detective McCarl had no time to arrest petty criminals. He had to find Doctor Boggo.

"Let's go and find this warehouse," he growled.

The two detectives made their way through the streets until they reached the abandoned warehouse. They knew it was the abandoned warehouse because there was a big sign outside that said 'abandoned warehouse'. They hid behind a lamppost and watched as two piglins in gold armor came out of the door and disappeared down a side street.

Piglins

"Looks like this is the place," said McCarl.

Alex nodded and pulled out two netherite swords. McCarl had his trusty crossbow.

"Let's do this," said McCarl.

The two of them sneaked over to the warehouse. One of the windows had broken glass, so they climbed inside it, being careful to be as quiet as possible. Detective McCarl had spent ten years training as a ninja, so he was an expert at sneaking around.

Inside were lots of machines that had once been used to turn iron ore into iron ingots, but they were now abandoned and covered in cobwebs. A few piglins with gold swords were hanging around, most of them sitting down on the ground. In the middle of the warehouse was an obsidian frame with a glowing purple force field in the center of it.

"A nether portal," whispered McCarl, as he and McAlex hid behind some barrels. "So that's where Doctor Boggo is hiding — the Nether."

Carl, I've got a question.

Okay, what is it?

Isn't it a bit obvious that Doctor Boggo and the piglins would be coming from the Nether? I mean, that's where piglins come from.

Well, er... Because it's so obvious, the audience won't be expecting it. That's what's clever about it.

Ah wow. You really are a great writer, Carl!

Thanks. Anyway, let me carry on with the story...

Detective McCarl surveyed the scene. He guessed there were about ten piglins in total. As McCarl was a ninja master, ten piglins would be no problem for him. He put his crossbow back in its sheath. He wouldn't be needing it.

"Now stay here," he whispered to McAlex. "It's time for me to make some porkchops."

"Shouldn't we wait until we're off duty to have dinner?" McAlex asked.

McCarl put his head in his hands. "I'm not actually going to make porkchops; I'm going to beat up all the piglins."

"Oh. But what do piglins have to do with porkchops? I don't think piglins drop porkchops when they're destroyed."

"Yes," said McCarl, "but pigs do."

"But what do pigs have to do with piglins?"

"Well, piglins are like pigs. The word pig is part of the word piglin."

"Oh right," said McAlex. "Do you know, I never made the connection between pigs and piglins before. You're very clever, Detective McCarl."

"Thanks," said McCarl. He pulled up his sleeves and then walked out from behind the barrels into the center of the warehouse. All the piglins turned to look at him, grunting angrily and equipping their gold swords.

"Right," grinned McCarl. "Who wants some?"

"I'll have some, please," said McAlex from behind the barrels. "Some what?"

"Can you just stay there and be quiet?" shouted McCarl.

"Can do," said McAlex.

Now that Detective McAlex had given away her position, the piglins were looking at her too. Some piglins had been hidden from view by crates, so there were more of them than Carl had thought. He and Alex stood back-to-back as the piglins surrounded them. They pulled out their swords and prepared to fight.

"You guys have made a *pig* mistake messing with us," growled McCarl.

"Great joke, Detective McCarl," said McAlex. "Instead of the word big, you used the word pig because they're piglins. That's really clever."

Then the piglins rushed towards them, and the battle began.

CHAPTER SIX

Fight!

Carl?

What is it, Alex?

Can I write the fight scene with the piglins?

No.

Puh-leeeeeeeeeeeeeeeeeeeeeeeeeeease?"

I said no.

PUH-LEEEEEEEEEEEEEEEEEEEEEEEEEEEEEEAAAASE???????

Okay, okay. But you'd better not make it stupid.

I promise, Carl. It won't be stupid at all.

SMASH! Suddenly two horses with wings flew through the window, and both McAlex and McCarl jumped onto their backs.

"We have come to help you, as we're very friendly horses," said one of the horses.

"Thanks, Mr Horse," said McAlex.

"Yeah, thanks, horses," said McCarl. "You're our best friends, and we love you very much!"

Erm, Alex, maybe I should still do the dialogue for Detective McCarl.

Okay, Carl, that's fine with me.

Suddenly more flying horses burst through the windows, but these ones were evil with glowing red eyes. The piglins jumped onto the evil horses' backs, and an awesome fight took place, with loads of horses flying around and cool things happening. Detective McCarl and McAlex were winning the fight, but after a while, they weren't winning the fight anymore.

"Oh no," said McAlex. "We were winning the fight, but now we're not winning the fight anymore! What shall we do?"

"We have to keep fighting!" shouted McCarl. "Let's show these piglins who's boss!"

So then more fighting took place, and it was really exciting with lots of ool things happening. Sometimes one side was winning the fight, and other imes the other side was winning the fight.

Alex, don't you think you should put a bit more detail into this battle?

What do you mean, Carl?

Well, you can't just say that one side was winning the fight; you have to how us. Show us exactly what's happening. All the gritty parts of the battle. Vhat weapons are they using? Are people getting injured? Are people etting killed?

Okay, Carl, I'll try...

The fight continued. Detective McCarl and one of the piglins were sword ighting. The piglin had a gold sword, and Detective McCarl had a netherite word. Detective McCarl swung at the piglin, and the piglin blocked it. Then he piglin swung at McCarl, and McCarl blocked it. Then McCarl swung at the iglin, and the piglin blocked it. Then the piglin swung at McCarl, and McCarl locked it. Then McCarl swung at the piglin —

Alex!!! Why are you making the battle so boring? You can't just have hem swinging swords at each other forever!

Sorry, Carl. I was just trying to make the battle more detailed.

Look, just write it however you want. I can edit out all your stupid stuff ater.

Yay! Thanks, Carl...

The battle raged on, with loads of epic fighting happening, with swords lashing and other stuff like that. It looked like McCarl and McAlex were oing to lose the battle, but suddenly the roof blasted open, and Pigzilla was here, staring down at them.

ROOOOOOOOOOOOOOOOOOOOOOOOAAAAAAARRRR!!!!!! said Pigzilla.

"I think he's saying that he's come here to help us against the piglins," aid McAlex. "Thank you, Pigzilla!"

Then Pigzilla got onto a flying horse and flew around, attacking the piglins. Before long, all the piglins were knocked out, and the battle was won.

"Thank you, Pigzilla!" said McAlex.

ROOOOOOOOOOOOOOOOOOOOOOOOAAAAAAARRRR!!!!!! said Pigzilla.

"I think he's saying that he has to go back to his home planet now," said McAlex. "Goodbye, Pigzilla!"

Then Pigzilla flew on his flying horse and flew off to the moon, which was where he lived.

"Well, that was a bit strange," said McCarl. "Shall we go into the Nether portal now?"

"Yeah, let's do it," said McAlex.

Alex, now that the battle is over do you mind if I take over the writing again?

Sure, Carl.

Detective McCarl and McAlex climbed off their flying horses. All the lying horses flew away and never came back into the story ever again. McCarl and McAlex walked up to the Nether portal.

"I never thought I'd be going back to the Nether again," growled McCarl. "Not after the last time."

"Don't you mean you *Nether* thought you'd be going back again," grinned McAlex.

"Very good," said McCarl, rolling his eyes.

"I made a joke!" said McAlex happily.

"Aren't you going to ask me about the last time I went to the Nether?" asked McCarl.

"Oh, okay," said McAlex. "What happened the last time you went to the Nether?"

"I don't want to talk about it."

"Oh, right, then why did you ask me to — "

"Okay, if you insist, I'll tell you. The last time I went to the Nether, I fought Doctor Boggo. I defeated him — or at least I thought I had – but it came at a terrible cost."

"Oh no, how many emeralds did it cost you?"

"It didn't cost me emeralds; it cost me my partner! Detective Nitwit and I graduated from police academy together. We were partners for years, but then, in the final battle with Doctor Boggo, Nitwit fell into a river of lava."

"Oh dear," said McAlex. "Was he okay?"

"Er, no," said Carl.

"I'm sorry to hear that," said McAlex.

"At least now I can get my revenge on Doctor Boggo once again," said McCarl. "I don't know how he survived last time, but this time I'm going to put an end to him once and for all."

Detective McCarl gritted his teeth. Because he was so incredibly manly, he didn't cry, but he still felt lots of emotion. He was a complex character with lots of layers. He took a deep breath and then stepped through the portal into the Nether.

CHAPTER SEVEN

Storming the Castle

They walked through the portal and found themselves in a Nether wastes biome, with endless netherrack hills in every direction and a huge lava lake in the distance. At first, Detective McCarl didn't spot anything unusual, then he saw a gigantic black castle in the middle of the lava, with a black bridge leading across to it.

"That must be Doctor Boggo's new base," McCarl growled. "Let's go pay him a visit."

"But how are we going to get past all those guards outside?" asked McAlex, pointing to a huge group of piglins in ninja outfits who were guarding the bridge.

"Follow my lead," said McCarl, putting on a pair of sunglasses. He walked down towards the bridge, with McAlex following on his heels. When they got to the bridge, all the Ninja piglins pointed their crossbows at them.

"Where your ID card?" one of the piglins asked. "No come in without ID card."

"I've got your ID card right here," said McCarl, reaching into his jacket and pulling out a bazooka. All the piglins squealed and began to run back across the bridge towards the castle.

"Special delivery," said McCarl. "First class!" Then DOOM, DOOM, DOOM, he pulled the trigger on the bazooka and fired TNT at the piglins.

"I didn't know you had a bazooka on you," said McAlex.

"I always like to keep a little something up my sleeve," grinned McCarl.

Suddenly they heard a swooshing sound above and looked up to see more ninja piglins flying down towards them with elytra wings. Detective McCarl didn't even miss a beat and pulled out another bazooka. This one fired swords, and as the piglins were hit by the swords, they fell down into the lava.

"I've heard of taking a hot bath, but this is ridiculous," grinned McCarl.

Carl?

Let me guess, Alex, you don't think it's very nice that Detective McCarl made all the piglins fall into the lava?

That's right. Could they survive somehow? Maybe they can have lava-proof ninja suits.

Sigh, okay, okay...

On the far bank of the lava lake, McCarl and McAlex saw the piglin ninjas crawling out from the lava. They all seemed to be okay.

NINJA PiGLiNS!

"I guess they must have lava-proof ninja suits," said McCarl. "Although that does seem to be a pretty stupid idea."

"Thank goodness they're okay," said McAlex happily.

McCarl and McAlex made their way across the bridge towards the castle. Thanks to McCarl's bazooka, there were gaps in the bridge, but McCarl jumped into the air and fired the rocket launcher down at the ground to launch himself over the gaps; in an epic move he called a rocket jump. Since McAlex didn't have her own bazooka, she had to use blocks to build her way across the bridge, as she wasn't as cool as Detective McCarl.

Inside the castle, more piglin ninjas were waiting for them. McCarl and McAlex fought the ninjas off with their swords, gradually making their way higher and higher in the castle. Finally, they came to a large chamber at the top of the castle. In the middle of the chamber was a huge glass box packed full of thousands of potatoes. McCarl's mouth dropped open.

"Potatoes..." He gasped happily.

"Potatoes belong to Boggo now," said a voice. McCarl turned around to see his old nemesis, Doctor Boggo. Doctor Boggo was a piglin in a long white lab coat and a monocle.

"So, we meet again," McCarl snarled. "How did you survive the last time, Boggo?"

Doctor Boggo chuckled, and when he spoke again, his voice had completely changed:

"I'm afraid you've been tricked, old chap," he said. "I'm not Doctor Boggo."

Then he reached up and pulled off a mask. Underneath the mask was a face that Carl knew all too well.

It was Chief Porkins.

CHAPTER EIGHT

Potatogeddon

Wow, Carl, what a great twist! So Chief Porkins was Dr Boggo all along, who would have thought?

No, Alex, you've got it the wrong way round. Doctor Boggo was Chief Porkins all along.

So, it was Chief Porkins who Carl pushed into lava all those years ago?

No, that was Doctor Boggo.

But I thought Chief Porkins was Doctor Boggo?

No, that was the actual Doctor Boggo. But he did die in the lava, and this is Chief Porkins pretending to be Doctor Boggo.

My brain hurts, Carl.

Listen, it's not that complicated! There was a real Doctor Boggo, but he died, and now Chief Porkins has been pretending to be Doctor Boggo.

But why was Chief Porkins pretending to be Doctor Boggo?

Because he's a secret bad guy. If you shut up and let me continue writing, I'll explain everything.

Please do, Carl. Because at the moment I don't really understand it.

Can I get on with the story now?

Oh, sorry, of course you can, Carl.

Thank you...

"Chief!" said McCarl. "So, you're the one behind the potato theft? Why? Why would you do such a terrible thing?"

"For revenge," said Chief Porkins. "When I was a young chap, everyone said I was the coolest police officer in Awesomeville. But then you came along, Detective McCarl, and you stole my thunder. Now everyone is saying that you're the best police officer, and my legacy is being forgotten. So now I'm taking all these potatoes — every single potato in the world – and I'm going to combine them all together into one giant potato. What do you think about that?"

"Actually, that sounds pretty great," said McCarl.

Chief Porkins snarled. "You think you're so cool, don't you, Detective McCarl? Just because you wear several pairs of sunglasses at once and everyone thinks you're amazing. Well, old bean, I haven't told you the best part of my plan yet. Once all the potatoes have been combined into a giant potato, I'm going to destroy it. And then there will be no more potatoes ever again!"

"Wow," said McAlex. "That's one strange plan, Chief."

"So, what do you think, Detective McCarl?" Chief Porkins asked with a grin. "Pretty good plan, ay, old chap?"

McCarl pulled out his bazooka and aimed it at Chief Porkins. But Chief Porkins just smiled and stepped in front of the glass tank.

"If you blow me up, you'll blow all the potatoes up as well, dear boy."

McCarl snarled angrily.

"Well, chaps, this has been fun," said Chief Porkins, "but now it's time for potatogeddon!

Ooo, Carl, Potatogeddon would have been a better title for this book.

What's wrong with World War Potato?

Well, there aren't really any wars in the book, and we don't see the whole world.

Listen, Alex, the title sounds cool, and that's the most important thing. If you have a cool title, people will buy the book.

Good thinking, Carl. You're really good at this book-writing thing.

I know I am. Now let me get on with this...

Chief Porkins quickly turned and tapped some buttons on the keypad. Immediately, all the potatoes in the glass chamber began swirling around and around and merged into a giant potato the size of a house. The entire castle began to shake.

"By the way, chaps, I forgot to tell you the best part of my plan," grinned Chief Porkins. "I'm going to destroy the giant potato... by dropping it on the city of Awesomeville! Those poor fools are going to pay for thinking that you're cooler than I am. Ha ha ha ha ha ha!"

He pressed another button, and there was a flash of purple. Both Chief

Porkins and the giant potato disappeared, leaving nothing but the empty glass chamber behind.

"Where did he go?" McAlex asked.

"He's gone back to the Overworld," growled McCarl. He ran over to the control panel. One of the buttons was purple and had the word 'Overworld' written on it. Carl slammed the button with his fist. There was a flash of purple light, and the next moment he and Detective McAlex were on the roof of a skyscraper, back in the overworld.

"Look up in the sky!" shouted McAlex.

McCarl looked up and saw a huge meteor plummeting through the sky, heading straight towards the city of Awesomeville. And then he realized it wasn't a meteor — it was the giant potato.

"Ha ha ha ha ha ha ha!"

McCarl turned and saw Chief Porkins standing behind them on the rooftop.

"There's nothing you can do, chaps," Chief Porkins shouted. "When that potato lands, Awesomeville will be obliterated."

"The only thing that's gonna be obliterated is your face," said McCarl. He jumped across the rooftop and did a karate kick, knocking Chief Porkins out.

"Hurray, you saved the day, Detective McCarl!" said McAlex.

"Er, don't forget the giant potato that's about to destroy the city," said McCarl.

"Oh yeah."

McCarl pulled out his bazooka and fired some TNT at the giant potato, but the potato was so big that the explosion barely made a dent in it.

"What are we going to do now?" asked McAlex.

"I don't know," said Detective McCarl, through gritted teeth. "I just don't know!"

Er, Alex?

Yes, Carl

Um... Do you have any idea how the two detectives can stop the giant potato?

Oh, didn't you want to write that bit, Carl?

Well, it's just... I can't think of a good ending. I was just going to have them shoot the giant potato with the bazooka, but that seems too simple. Do you have any ideas?

Oh yes, I've got some really good ideas, Carl!

Are you sure? You're not just gonna write something stupid again?

What do you mean 'again'? Didn't you like my bit with the flying horses?

Er... It was great. Look, just write something, will you? And please don't make me regret this.

Don't worry, Carl — I'll come up with something really cool!

The giant potato sped down towards the ground. In a few seconds, it would destroy the entire city, but thankfully, Junior Detective McAlex had a ool plan up her sleeve.

"Redstone mech, activate!" she shouted.

Suddenly a giant robot mech suit came flying through the sky towards er. Alex jumped into the mech and took control of it. Then a second giant obot suit came flying through the air, and Detective McCarl jumped into hat.

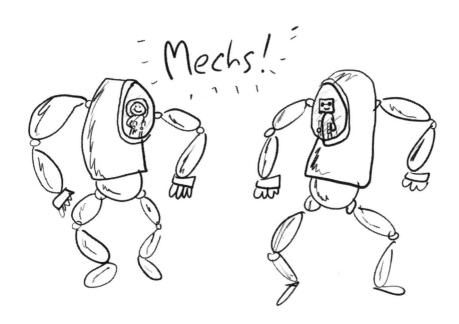

"We need to combine our mechs to make a super mech!" shouted McAlex. "It's the only way to defeat the giant potato!"

"Er, okay..." said McCarl.

McAlex's mech and McCarl's mech both combined, forming one single ig mech.

"Now let's bash that potato's butt!" said McAlex.

"Wait!" said McCarl. "That giant potato contains every single potato in the world. If we destroy it, there won't be any more potatoes!"

"Then there's only one thing for it," said McAlex. "We need to absorb the power of the giant potato... and turn the entire city into potato!"

McAlex fired the mech's absorption ray at the giant potato. The giant potato disappeared, and all the potato energy was sucked into the mech. The mech rose up into the sky, glowing with yellow energy.

"YAAAAAAAAAAAAAAAAAAAAAAAAAAAHHHHHHHHHHHHHHHHH H!!!!!!!!!!!!!!!!!!!!" McAlex yelled.

"YAAAAAAAAAAAAAAAAAAAAAAAAAAAAAAAAAAAAAAAAAAAAAAAAA AAAAAAAAAAAAAAAAAAAAAAAAAAAAAAAAAAAAAAAAAAAAAAAAAAA AAAAAAAAAAAAAAAAAAAAAAAAAAAAAAAAAAAAAAAAAAAAAAAAAA AAHHHHHHHHHHHHHHHHHHHHHHHHHHHHHHHHHHHHHHHHHHH HHHHHH!!!"

Er, Alex, what's going on?

The mech has absorbed the giant potato.

Right... Well, get on with it then. Let's see the ending you've come up with.

You won't be disappointed, Carl! Right, here goes...

Once the mech was fully charged with potato energy, Alex turned the absorption ray down towards the ground and put it in reverse. Potato energy shot out of the ray, hitting the ground, and a wave of potato energy spread throughout the city. When the dust cleared, the entire city of Awesomeville, all the buildings and streets, were now made from potato.

The mech broke apart, and McAlex and McCarl fell back onto the roof of the building.

"What's going on?" Chief Porkins said groggily. He'd just woken up from being knocked out.

"We defeated you, you idiot," said McCarl.

"And we've turned the city into potato," said McAlex.

"Nice one, Alex," grinned Detective McCarl. "Now, the people of Awesomeville will never run out of potatoes ever again. We can eat baked potatoes for every meal."

A single happy tear rolled down his cheek. Detective McCarl was normally so manly that he never cried, but seeing his beloved city turned into potato overwhelmed him.

McCarl and McAlex brought Chief Porkins to jail, and then they went to join the celebrations. The people of Awesomeville were throwing a huge party in the streets, with everyone eating as much potato as they could.

"Three cheers for detective McCarl and junior detective McAlex!" someone shouted. And everyone cheered three times.

After the party had finished, the two detectives sat on the rooftop, watching the sun go down.

"You did good today, partner," Detective McCarl growled.

"Thanks," said McAlex happily.

"And to reward you for all you've done, I'm promoting you... to senior detective," said McCarl.

"Do you have the authority to do that?" asked McAlex.

McCarl grinned. "You know me, I don't play by the rules."

Then they both laughed: ha ha ha ha ha ha ha ha ha ha!

The end.

Okay, Alex, I'll admit — that was a pretty good ending. I wouldn't mind living in a city made from potato.

I'm glad you liked it, Carl. Well, I guess that's our book finished. Now what?

Now we need to bring it to a printer and get it turned into a proper book. Then we can sell it and make our fortune. If I make enough emeralds, maybe I can build a real-life city made from potato.

And maybe I can build a real-life city made from cake!

Don't be ridiculous, Alex.

Sorry, Carl. Anyway, it's been fun writing this book with you.

You too, Alex. But let's never, ever, ever do it again...

THE (REAL) END

Printed in Great Britain
by Amazon

13470054R00036